HOW TO MAKE
PESACH IN FIVE DAYS

MOSAICA PRESS

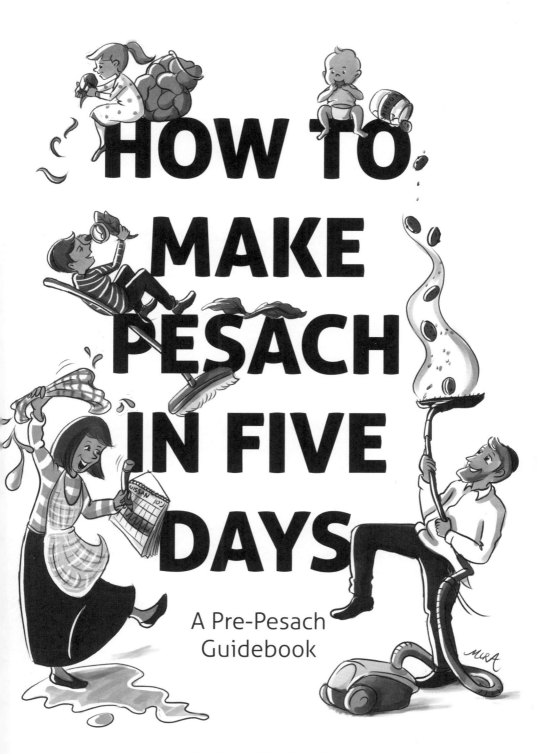

HOW TO MAKE PESACH IN FIVE DAYS

A Pre-Pesach Guidebook

Meira Spivak

Table of Contents

Acknowledgments

THANK YOU to my husband, Rabbi Chanan Spivak, who puts up with all my grand ideas and picks up the slack where I fall short. A man of great kindness, he is an incredible role model for all who know him.

Thank you to my children, who join in the fun and help make the 5-day pre-Pesach experience positive and enjoyable. I couldn't make Pesach without you!

Thank you to my parents, who have demonstrated what a clean home should look like, and to my mom, who provided the scrumptious recipes in this book. I can't wait to make them each year. Thank you to my siblings, who make Pesach cleaning a humorous experience.

Thank you to my in-laws, who have welcomed us for Pesach so often, and my sisters- and brothers-in-law, who have let us invade their homes countless times! Your patience knows no end.

Thank you to Dovid Bashevkin and Shari Weisenberg of the Orthodox Union, who have helped with this work from the onset, giving their time, wisdom, and expertise. I also thank the entire NCSY and OU teams, who have helped make this book a reality.

Thank you to Amy R. Kaufman, a judicious editor whose advice has been invaluable.

Before You Start, Read This

FOR MANY OF US, preparing for Pesach involves a lot of work and worry. This book is intended to take away the worry and simplify the work.

Some people start worrying about Pesach months in advance. Nightmares, cold sweats, endless to-do lists…all this amounts to worrying about worrying. It's true, the work can be a bit frenzied at times, but with this book you can create a serene, joyful Pesach in just five days—without making everyone crazy.

To be totally honest, I'm not saying you don't have to *think* about Pesach until five days beforehand. I've divided the book into three parts, to be read in the order you choose.

- Part I is a blueprint for cleaning and cooking for the entire holiday in 5 days. (It's a marathon.) With proper planning and focus, it *can* be done!
- Part II takes care of all the other details, from inviting the guests to arranging for a babysitter. (*A word of advice:* Handle this part beginning the day after Purim, and you'll be in great shape for the marathon.)
- Part III includes basic recipes and some all-important sample lists to be used as a resource.

This book has been years in the making, but I didn't formally sit down to write it until 2020. (*Note:* This work is not intended to be a halachic source. For guidance on what is right for you, please reach out to your personal rabbi.) The idea began to take shape when I took my son to the doctor for his annual checkup. He dreads vaccines, and before the appointment, his anxiety level began to rise. When doomsday came, he hid in the bushes. I removed the thorns from his hair and bribed him to get into the car, never once losing my cool (cough-cough). After sitting tensely in the waiting room, the nurse came in, and we had heavy tears. And then, after 0.1 second per shot, a sense of calm came over the room. We had made it to the other side.

Reflecting on this experience, I realized that many of us have pre-Pesach scenarios similar to this. We panic long before we need to and go through stages of denial and avoidance, all in fear of the big day. That was when I asked myself, "What is the point of being stressed out for weeks and months before when you can have it all done in five days?"

Welcome to *How to Make Pesach in 5 Days*. This book presents ideas that you can easily incorporate into your family's routine. Your mind will not be cluttered with details—the organizing and scheduling has been done for you. You will plan and you will prepare, but no more will you stress. You will come into the Seder rested and relaxed, ready to pass on the torch to the next generation. As you look around at the beautifully dressed table, you will feel the greatest sense of accomplishment. When you follow this guide faithfully, you and your family may look forward to "the 5 Days" with eager anticipation.

HOW THIS BOOK CAME ABOUT

For the last few years, I have been giving pre-Pesach webinars to help women prepare for Pesach. I'm a pretty organized person (*read:* my house is a wreck), and I'm a great multitasker (*read:* I can't do anything well). I am a type A who loves tackling huge projects head on. So, I figured Pesach was a great place to start.

Honestly, my Pesach prep wasn't always stress-free—in fact, it used to be just plain overwhelming. One year, an NCSY Shabbaton landed very close to Pesach. Since a caterer is not always available in our small Jewish community, we often cook for the entire Shabbaton ourselves. This meant that not only would I need to clean my home for Pesach, but in the middle of it all, I'd have to cook five meals for eighty of my closest friends.

Since there were about four weeks till Pesach, I had a choice. Would I spend the entire time cleaning and stressing out over Pesach, and in the midst of the chaos, spend two weeks working on the Shabbaton? Or would I concentrate on the Shabbaton for the first two weeks and risk preparing for Pesach closer to the holiday? I chose the latter, and it was one of the best decisions I ever made. You see, in previous years I would clean a room two weeks before Pesach, only to turn around and find Cheerios strewn all over the floor. It's frustrating to think you have finished a job, only to find out that you need to do it again. And again. And again. But no more. I will not clean in advance only to have it destroyed!

In caring for a large family, I have become quite an expert in the ways one's work can be done and undone. I hope this book will help you laugh at the stresses and embrace the joys of preparing for Pesach.

Wishing you an incredible Nissan!

Meira

PART I

The 5 Days: Cleaning and Cooking— It *Can* Be Done!

There is ample room for creativity within these five days. You may choose to spend more time cooking than cleaning and vice versa. I have estimated two and a half days for each project, but feel free to adjust the plan to your lifestyle.

CLEANING (2.5 DAYS)

You will be cleaning *everything* in this brief whirlwind. The goal is to *kasher* and turn over your kitchen and be ready to begin cooking by the end of the first two and a half days.

Wash Your Car

You basically have four options on this one:

- Bring it to a professional company and have your car vacuumed or even detailed.
- Have a professional company detail your car in the comfort of your own driveway.
- Clean it yourself, either at the pay-as-you-go section of your local car wash or in your driveway.

- Bring it to the local charity car wash and then clean it again after the "cleaners" are done. (As somebody who runs a charity car wash each year, I hope you'll choose the last option.)

Windex

Don't even think about cleaning until you have bought a ton of cleaning products and paper towels. Keep a product like Windex on hand.

Remember, we are not aiming to *remove* every crumb of chametz—that is nearly impossible, and nobody's got time for that! However, a whole entity of chametz, no matter how small, cannot remain in our possession, so Cheerios are a major threat. You are bound to come in contact with chametz that is hard to remove, and by spraying it with a poisonous cleaning solution and rendering it unfit to be eaten, even by a dog, you have nullified the chametz from your possession (oukosher.org). Bring your Windex with you as you go from room to room, and as you encounter hard-to-reach pieces of chametz, spray them until they are inedible, and then move on.

If your home has already been spring-cleaned (see Part II, "Spring-Cleaning"), cleaning the rooms will seem almost simple. You will know the rooms well and understand what the cleaning job entails. Nevertheless, a lot of junk will have accumulated, so there will still be work to do.

How to Clean Your Home

Before I clean, a thought is fixed in my mind, and I repeat it as a mantra: *Chametz represents the ego, and I need to work on removing it.* I remind myself that my focus in life should be on making the right choices, and I should try not to let my ego get in the way of doing what's right. You may want to adopt your own phrase.

As you embark on cleaning, here are a few rules to follow. Go from room to room. Set a timer with the minimum time you will need to clean a particular room. Put on fast music and commit to not schmoozing on the phone as you clean. The 5 Days are a time to be at one with yourself and not to start calling every last friend from seminary and wishing them a good Yom Tov. If you want this system to work, you need to be totally focused. It's hard, but you'll reap the rewards later.

The Toys

As you approach the toys, make a quick decision. Discard them, lock them up, or clean them. I'd suggest locking up most of them and including them in your *mechiras chametz*. If you decide to clean them, here are some options:

- Lay them on the floor, spray with Windex, and clean them.
- Put them in a bathtub with soapy water, rinse, and air dry.
- If the toy is washable, place it in a pillowcase and tie it with a knot. Wash on the gentle cycle of your washing machine and then air dry. I do this with Mega Bloks and it works perfectly.

If you are not sure what to discard, use the following axiom—when in doubt, throw it out! It works wonders. You shouldn't have too many decisions to make at this point, since you probably threw things out during spring-cleaning (see Part II for more on this optional task).

The Beds

Remove all linen from the bed, and shake it out for crumbs. I usually wash the linen, because I like our home to feel fresh and clean for Pesach. If you wash all the linen in the house, keep in mind this will occupy your washing machines for most of the day. If you have kids, you may want to lift up the mattresses and check underneath. I find incredible amounts of chametz in the cracks of the beds, including Cheerios, noodle soups, pretzels, crackers, candy, and chocolate.

Next, move the beds and check behind them. Although you might not think anyone would eat behind their beds, you are unequivocally wrong. Little boys will. Maybe little girls too.

Furniture

Move all moveable furniture and sweep behind. You need not clean underneath any furniture or appliance that cannot be moved out of its place (such as a breakfront, refrigerator, or built-in appliance). Inaccessible chametz is automatically *batel* (oukosher.org). Open all drawers and lift the contents to search for chametz and then put them back in. Remember, you are not refolding clothing now or organizing your junk drawers. This was done a few weeks ago during spring-cleaning (again, see Part II for more on this optional task). Just open the drawers, lift the items, scan and return. Continue until you've done the entire room. Check clothing pockets and closet floors. Check the laundry basket, as apparently Cheerios are often stored in them. Books for adults do not need to be checked, but be careful not to bring them to the table on Pesach (oukosher.org). When you are finished cleaning the furniture, sweep and mop the room.

If You Have Boys

If you have boys in your family, you have an additional game to play. It's called "If I were a hoarder, where would I hoard things?" Get into the mind of your eight-year-old. Check for chametz on windowsills, inside board games, among their baseball card and assorted other collections. In short, any place where you would never put chametz, check.

The Couch

I will never forget the day we moved from our apartment in Israel. Although we were only moving one block, we decided to sell our couches. Picture the scene. Two men walk in to examine and buy the couches. They pay for them and proceed to lift up one couch, but as they approach the door, they need to turn the couch upside down and angle it out. Well, you can imagine their surprise (and ours) when basically our entire lives fell out of the couch. My missing keys, spare change, important papers, kids' yarmulkes, you name it. I was so embarrassed that I couldn't stop laughing, and to this day I remember the scene when cleaning the couch for Pesach.

The couch is extremely difficult—plus it cannot be included in the *mechiras chametz* if you plan on using it. I even tried suggesting that we buy a new couch each year, *l'kavod yom tov* of course, but my husband didn't go for it. As you clean, turn the couch upside down and watch the treasures fall out. Check every crack, sticking your hand down as far as it will go, and bring the Windex with you. I'd definitely suggest wearing gloves for this project.

Your Garage—or Any Area Used for Storage

Ahh, everyone's favorite job—the garage. Let's divide this category into two types of garages:

A. The garage that is spotless and is actually used to house cars.
B. The garage that is packed with stored food and supplies, including extra refrigerators and freezers, children's bikes, tools, paper goods from Costco, spare tables and chairs, a lawn mower, broken items that might one day be fixed, toys, old clothing you planned to save for another child, rodent traps, tablecloths and centerpieces you might need for a *simchah*, and sukkah boards.

If you own garage A, feel free to clean it, as it will probably take about ten minutes. If you own garage B, I'd suggest clearing off a few shelves and cleaning them for Pesach, if you need the space for extra Pesach goods. Then cover the rest and include in your *mechiras chametz*. (Reach out to your own rabbi to determine the most fitting procedure for your family.) It's too late to clean the entire garage. If you still would like it cleaned, I wish you the best of luck, and I give you a *berachah* of immense *shalom bayis*.

Cleaning and Other Help

Although you are still proud of yourself for having made Pesach without a cleaning lady during the 2020 pandemic, please hire cleaning help if it's safe to do so (this should be arranged prior to the 5 Days). Delegate the worst jobs to them (ovens, fridges, and the like), or even jobs you just don't like (cleaning out and lining the drawers). If you can, bring back the help during the cooking stages, so your house won't look like a war zone when you are done. Please also confirm that your babysitters/spouse/older kids will be available to help with upcoming tasks.

Remember, do not use hot water in the kitchen sinks for twenty-four hours before you plan to *kasher*. Keep this in mind as you clean, and advise your cleaning person of this too.

Kitchen Cabinets

How many cabinets should you clean out and use for Pesach? Opinions differ. The minority opinion says to clean out and line just a few basic cabinets and drawers, and keep extra products in the garage or on specially built plastic Pesach shelves. The majority opinion says to empty out every cabinet in your kitchen until you have more shelves than you will ever need for Pesach. Going with the majority will allow you to place each Pesach serving bowl on its own shelf (ahh, space…), while adopting the minority view will leave you feeling extremely frustrated. (Unless you are a minimalist, your counter will become a dumping ground.) I advise reaching a happy medium.

Kashering

Once you are finished cleaning the kitchen, it is ready to be *kashered*. Although the laws of this process are beyond the scope of this work, here is a brief list of things you'll want to remember. For more information on how to *kasher* your kitchen, take a look at oukosher.org.

Either (1) *kasher* or (2) close up the following:

Ovens
Cooktops
Countertops
Sinks
Microwaves
Dishwashers
Cabinets
Pantry

Shopping

If you haven't ordered your fresh vegetables and fruit for delivery, be sure to shop for them during the first two and a half days. Having the ingredients on hand will make the cooking much smoother.

Shopping will be much easier if you review "Make Your Menu" and "Sample Menus" in Part II and "Sample Shopping List" in Part III.

Bring Out Your Pesach Supplies

Once your kitchen is *kashered*, it's time to bring out your mixers, peelers, knives, and other Pesach kitchen supplies, so you'll be ready to cook first thing in the morning. I like to bring everything out, including Pesach dishes and serving ware, and put them in their assigned places.

If you have a huge amount of Pesach stuff, taking it all out at once may be overwhelming; at a minimum, be ready with your basic cooking utensils for tomorrow.

Cooking List

Take a few minutes to sit down and reflect on all your hard work. You have successfully cleaned your house in two and a half days! That's amazing!

Now sit down with a piece of paper and list the foods you plan to cook on each of the remaining two and a half days. Assign a day and time for every item on your menu for every day of Pesach.

I will be referring to the two sets of special days of Pesach. "The first days" means the first two days of Pesach; "the second days" refers to the last two days. If you would like to wait until *erev* the second days to prepare certain foods, make a separate list for this as well.

For example:

Tuesday
9:00 a.m.
Chicken soup
11:00 a.m.
Brisket
3:00 p.m.
Hasselback potatoes

Please guard these papers with your life. I repeat, do not accidentally discard these papers. Hide them far from your kids and do not write the lists on a napkin. These lists will guide your next two and a half days of prep.

Remember, if you haven't finished cleaning or turning over your kitchen, continue cleaning on your first day of cooking. You'll just need to cook faster.

My Cooking Schedule

My Cooking Schedule

My Cooking Schedule

COOKING (2.5 DAYS)

I have fond memories of peeling potatoes for my mother as we prepared for Pesach. With this guide, you will create wonderful memories for your family and guests.

First Day of Cooking

Before I start, I like to say an extra-special thank you to Hashem for allowing us to make Yom Tov without having to bake challahs also. I love challah as much as the next person, but not having to bake them is a major time-saver.

For most of this section, we will work backward. Anything that can be frozen will be made first, and the freshest items will be prepared last. The first day is basically designated for kugels and desserts, and we'll be whipping about a hundred eggs!

Desserts and Kugels

Begin with the kugels—all of them for the entire Pesach. I'd suggest making them in pans of various shapes so each kugel feels like a different experience. Have your kids peel apples and potatoes to make the kugel part go faster. Though they can only peel one apple for every ten of yours, it is still one less apple you have to peel!

Next, go on to all the main desserts (ice creams, mousses) and side desserts (cookies, biscotti). Keep in mind that you will need some *mezonos* cookies or cakes on hand for Kiddush, as well as baked goods for when the kids complain they are starving for the thousandth time.

Feel free to let the kids help; just be prepared for a mess afterward. I love having them hold the hand-held mixer while the egg whites are beating, but they usually don't stay with the task for long. (Better yet, invest in a stand mixer and have your kids peel all the potatoes!)

Packaging and Packing

After you have prepared each food, cover it with foil and/or place it directly in the Ziploc bag and put it away. Don't just write the contents on the top of the bag. My daughter came up with the ingenious idea of writing the name of the item on the side of the Ziploc, so when you open your freezer and see pans stacked on top of each other, you can read the name of the item without having to lift the pans.

Items going into the fridge do not need Ziplocs, but I advise you to put any messy items in a Ziploc as well.

And that's it for the first day of cooking. Go to bed early!

Second Day of Cooking

Today's focus will be the main dishes (meats, poultry, fish), cooked and roasted veggies, and soups.

The Proteins

I use this time to prepare fish, meat, poultry, and any other protein that will be needed for the entire Pesach. This can include turkey for a main dish, meatballs, and chicken for a grilled chicken salad. When preparing the meats, keep in mind that cooking them is only half the job. The other half is slicing them. I advise buying a good-quality electric meat slicer. Or you can do what I did—buy five cheap ones that break and have to be replaced with a good one. Your choice. Slice the meats, return them with their juices to the disposable pans, cover with heavy-duty foil, and place in Ziploc bags. Mark each bag with its contents and freeze.

The Sides/Appetizers

During this time, prepare all side dishes that must be made fresh for the first days. These can include roasted and fried vegetables, as well as all the variations of potatoes you can dream of. Appetizers made from potatoes can also be prepared now. Mashed potatoes can be frozen (as long as they are steaming when reheated), so you can also make your mock knish appetizers now.

The Soup

Don't forget to make your matzah balls or other soup accompaniments of your choice. I've always had a hard time making matzah balls from scratch, as we use *shemurah* matzah (think golf balls), but a few years ago I was given the perfect recipe (see p. 33). They come out terrific every time. I like to make matzah balls for the entire Pesach and pack them in tins and Ziplocs labeled with the meal and day/date. Right before the meals, I place the frozen matzah balls in the soup and heat them up together.

This is a lot of cooking, and you will probably be up late on this day. But remember, tomorrow is just half a day of work.

The Last Half-Day of Cooking/Erev Pesach

This is a lighter day of cooking in order to give you and your family time for naps before the Seder. Coming to the Seder as a rested human being is of the highest priority. Today, you will only need to make two types of food.

The Seder Plate

Prepare everything you need for the Seder plate, including the *charoses* and the *maror*. Make the salt water, cook the eggs, and roast the one egg and the shank bone. Check for bugs on all the lettuce (and fresh herbs) you will need. If you want to save time at the Seder, portion the lettuce (*maror*) in advance and place it in individual bags.

The Fresh Salads

This is the time to organize and prepare your fresh and marinated salads. For some salads, you can make just the dressing and place it in separate containers or Ziplocs, later filling them with vegetables to be marinated. For fresh salads, prepare the entire salad. If you are worried about preparing vegetables too early, place cut paper towels in the bag with your cut vegetables to extend their freshness. I sometimes cut the vegetables as much as two days in advance if I am concerned about time, and they always come out fine. *Please note:* You will need to do some prep of fresh vegetables and salads for the second days as they approach.

Mazal tov! You've finished Part I. Now go take a nap and wake up really feeling like royalty!

PART II

Getting Ready for the 5 Days: Be Happy, Not Harried

The weeks leading up to the 5 Days are the perfect time to do what I call "stress-free organizing." Here are some bits of practical wisdom that will pave the way for a smooth 5 Days. I would recommend starting these tasks when Purim ends.

SPRING-CLEANING

This is that special time of year when all of you neat freaks can go crazy. After Purim you are free to spring-clean for three weeks, twenty-four hours a day, six days a week. You can wash your curtains, dust your light bulbs, and clean the inside of your gutters. You can turn your mattresses, organize the contents of your medicine cabinet by date, and wipe down your moldings. It's true that you can spring-clean any time of year, but these three weeks are special—because as soon as they are over, you must cease from all spring-cleaning. I repeat—you may never spring-clean during the 5 Days! It's forbidden.

As you clean, feel your anxiety lowering and your stress levels dropping. If a child comes into the room and begins to ruin your work, just stop and move on to something else. No need to get upset or raise your voice. Remember, this is all bonus cleaning and shall be done in a calm and serene state.

As you get closer to the 5 Days, you will hear a voice inside you (or maybe the voice of a family member) insisting that you have to start the really stressful jobs already. The voice says, "Pesach is coming and there is no way you will finish on time." This is the voice of the *yetzer hara*. Do not listen to it. Do not give in. Commit to not stressing about Pesach until the latest possible moment.

MEAL PLANNING FOR THE 5 DAYS

Your family wouldn't like to eat potatoes and eggs for days before Pesach (see Part II, p. 22, section on potatoes). So, you'll need to give a little thought to what you will serve during the 5 Days when you are super focused on the main tasks. If pizza and bagel stores are open, terrific. If not, here are some practical ideas:

- Designate one area in your home to plug in a Crock-Pot, an Instapot, or sandwich makers so anyone can whip up a quick dinner.
- Pre-make dishes and freeze them so you can just reheat them later.
- If you have access to a barbecue, grill something for dinner.
- Eat in a nearby park.

You don't need a full menu plan, but just having these meals in the back of your mind will give you an advantage.

In some years the schedule is a little more complicated. Sometimes the 5 Days start on Shabbos (Hagadol). This means you're either going to count Thursday, or half Friday/half Motzaei Shabbos, as Day 1. Then you need to cook for Shabbos in the middle of all the cleaning and cooking. Come up with a strategy that works for you: Can you buddy up with a friend to divide the cooking, so each of you prepares a double meal and then you share the food? Can you order takeout that week or cook for the whole Shabbos in advance? Being prepared will leave you with the entire Friday to designate for Pesach preparation.

Make Your Menu

At this point you are either going to regret the past and change your ways, or you're going to think I'm a psychopath. You see, menu makers can be divided into two types—those who write their menus on the back of a paper plate or scraps of paper and those who keep them on Google docs. To be totally transparent, I do both. During the year for a regular Shabbos, I just write my menu anywhere and use it as a quick checklist while I cook everything on my list. It usually gets lost or discarded within ten minutes, but for the most part, I don't care—when I have finished cooking, I don't really need the list any more. This is definitely not true with Yom Tov menus.

I used to go about it all wrong. I'd write days' worth of Pesach meals on papers, only to lose them. Each year I'd have to start from scratch and try to remember what I served for the second lunch on Pesach two years ago. Of course, I never remembered, so I'd start from scratch and waste a lot of time. But no more!

After fifteen years of not noticing that my insanely organized family members kept their menus from year to year, I had an epiphany. Why should I reinvent the wheel every year when I could just duplicate and rename a Word doc from Pesach Menu 2020 to Pesach Menu 2021 and have an instant Pesach menu? Of course, I make a few changes. For instance, why do I keep making ratatouille when I'm the only one eating it? Or why am I making two different menus for both Sedarim when the second Seder is basically a repeat of the first one?

It's easier to cook large quantities of a single dish than to make a ton of different ones. To avoid repetition (serving potato kugel for several meals in a row), spread it out so the same food isn't served on consecutive nights. For example, you'll want to serve the same foods on the first and third days instead of twice on the first day.

Sample Menus

This sample menu provides plenty of variety and enough time to enjoy the process. Shabbos often occurs between the first days and the last days, so I've included a menu for ten meals.

If the item has a number after it, it means that dish will be served more than once. The numbers 1, 2, and 3 next to each dish reflect whether you're serving it for the first, second, or third time. Dishes served only once are not followed by a number.

First Days Meal 1 (Seder)
Chicken Soup 1
Brisket 1
Hasselback Potatoes 1
Grilled Vegetables 1
Chocolate Mousse Pie 1

First Days Meal 2 (Lunch)
Onion Soup 1
Spinach Salad 1
Coleslaw 1
Corned Beef 1
Onion Kugel 1
Mashed Potatoes 1
Rocky Road Brownies 1
Fruit Platter 1

First Days Meal 3 (Seder)
Chicken Soup 2
Brisket 2
Hasselback Potatoes 2
Grilled Vegetables 2
Chocolate Mousse Pie 2

First Days Meal 4 (Lunch)
Mock Potato Knishes 1
Deli Salad
Turkey
Vegetable Kugel
Roasted Cauliflower
Potato Wedges
Ice Cream 1
Brownies 1

Friday Night Meal 5
Chicken Soup 3
Salad with Grilled Vegetables
Roasted chicken
Meatballs
Potato Kugel 1
Ratatouille
Coffee Ice Cream

Shabbos Day Meal 6
Salmon/Gefilte Fish
Health Salad
Green Salad
Cholent
Potato Chip Schnitzel
Potato Kugel 2
Grilled Vegetables
Fruit Platter 1

Second Days Meal 1 (Dinner)	Second Days Meal 2 (Lunch)
Second Chicken Soup 4	Onion Soup 2
Coleslaw 2	Spinach Salad 2
Cucumber Salad 1	London Broil
Chicken in Wine	Mashed Potatoes 2
Fried Onion and Peppers	Onion Kugel 2
Potato Wedges 2	Ice Cream 2
Biscotti	Brownies 2
Chocolate Mousse	
Second Days Meal 3 (Dinner)	**Second Days Meal 4 (Lunch)**
Leftovers!	Mock Potato Knishes 2
	Cucumber Salad 2
	Corned Beef 2
	Chicken Nuggets
	Potato and Sweet Potato Fries
	Rocky Road Brownies 2
	Fruit Platter 2

Although you are serving some dishes more than once, your guests will feel they are eating a different dish every time. Whenever you cut potatoes into a different shape, you are in essence giving them a different experience. People pay for experiences, so do not underestimate the power of this statement. Since potatoes may be on the menu every day during Pesach, consider the infinite variations:

- Potato Kugel (see p. 35)
- Mashed Potatoes
- Mock Potato Knishes (Place mashed potatoes in a cup. Flip the cup upside down onto a cookie sheet, brush with egg. Bake at 350°.)
- Hasselback Potatoes (Make slits most of the way down the potato and fill the slits with garlic, salt, and oil. Bake at 350°.)
- Roasted Potatoes (potatoes cut into small pieces)
- Potato Wedges (potatoes cut into thick slices the long way)
- Potato Fries (potatoes and sweet potatoes cut into skinny strips like fries)
- Baked Potatoes (whole potatoes)
- Ridged Potatoes (potatoes cut into waffle-shaped fries with a potato-ridger)

I think you get the point. Your kids will never get sick of potatoes. And if they do, remind them that it is Pesach and, as Jews, we eat potatoes.

INVITE YOUR GUESTS

If you are *kiruv*-minded like I am, you'll probably want to invite a lot of guests for Yom Tov. If you're like me, you'll email people to join you for meals, most of whom won't respond. Then you'll sort through those who did respond affirmatively and place them at the meals that work best. This is actually a good thing, because if everyone responded, I'd be in big trouble.

I am also super picky about matching up my guests, so starting the invitation process early gives me a chance to do that. If you have your own kids, decide in advance which meals will be only for the family and don't invite others during that time. (There's no need to feel bad about saying no when people ask if they can join you for that meal—you're doing the right thing!)

Please note that you will not finalize your guest list until a few days before Yom Tov, but you must start in advance if you want this process to go smoothly.

Invitation List

First Days: Meal 1 (Seder)

First Days: Meal 2 (Lunch)

First Days: Meal 3 (Seder)

First Days: Meal 4 (Lunch)

Friday Night: Meal 5

Shabbos Day: Meal 6

Second Days: Meal 1 (Dinner)

Second Days: Meal 2 (Lunch)

Second Days: Meal 3 (Dinner)

Second Days: Meal 4 (Lunch)

CLOTHING

Switching Over Your Kids' Clothing

Don't pretend you have no idea what I'm talking about. Your kids have outgrown their current size, but it doesn't make sense to change over their clothing now because you know that the seasons will change again soon after Pesach. For example, your child is currently in a size 3T and he should have been moved to a 4T. Don't make him wear 3T clothing for another two months. Just switch over his clothing during this time. Now, for some of you, and you know who you are, your child is in a 3T and she is eight years old. For you—please don't wait. Change her clothes immediately.

For everyone else, now is the time to start switching over the clothing to the next season's attire, so when Chol Hamoed comes and it's warm outside, you won't be shocked that your kids have nothing to wear. Better to be shocked now, when you are able to deal with it.

Buying Your Pesach Clothing

This is perhaps the most daunting of tasks, so I will break it down into parts:

- Those of you with teen girls
- Everyone else

Or perhaps we can do an alternate breakdown:

- Those of you with teen girls who live out of town
- Everyone else

You see, until you have teen girls, this task seems pretty simple. You go to the local store or website and purchase the clothes your children need, and you are done. It's amazing. You have a need, you fill the need, and everyone is happy. You might even have to go to two stores or have one store special order the clothing, but you manage to outfit everyone.

Let me be honest with you—you don't have my sympathy! I have teen girls. You see, before my girls were teens, I thought I knew what the mitzvah of prayer was actually about. But apparently, I was wrong! I had previously thought that I needed to identify a need, turn to Hashem and ask Him for it, and wait to see what happened. It was only when

I had the opportunity to go shopping with my daughters that I was introduced to real prayer. Once I realized this task was harder than the splitting of the sea, I learned to say *Tehillim* before every shopping trip.

No matter what clothing I suggested, they didn't like it. No matter what opinion I had, it was wrong. If it didn't fit them, they thought it did. If it fit them, they thought it didn't. And to make matters worse, we live "out of town," and our shopping trips not only entailed *mazal* but also a level of prophecy. You see, as part of my job as chauffeur, I also needed to clearly envision what styles would be worn in New York for Pesach that year, so when the girls showed up for summer camp with those clothes, they wouldn't be completely shunned. Once I had spent a few minutes enveloped in prayer, I had to spend the next thirty minutes lying to them that the outfit on the mannequin in Target was exactly what the girls would be wearing in Lakewood for Pesach.

To put it simply, if you have younger kids, shopping for Pesach clothing might be a two- to three-hour activity. If you have teen girls, please allocate the entire three weeks!

In conclusion: If you're not totally spent, treat yourself to something nice to wear for Pesach.

Tailoring

Now that you've bought the clothes, you have the opportunity to discuss the mitzvah of modesty with your teenage daughters. Since this discussion doesn't always end positively, make sure to distract them while throwing the disputed garment discreetly into a garbage bag and head to the seamstress at once. Bring your boys'/men's suits as well!

Shaatnez Testing/Dry Cleaning

Bring your newly purchased clothes to the *shaatnez* tester to ensure that none of your new garments have both wool and linen thread. Then, if these or any other garments you have need cleaning, bring them to the dry cleaner. The dry cleaning should be done as close to the 5 Days as possible—after they've been worn the last time before Pesach—so they'll be fresh and clean for the holiday.

LINING SHELVES/BUYING DRY GOODS

During this time, you will also want to order your dry Pesach goods, such as oil and matzah. Make sure to clean off a section of shelves and line them properly so you have somewhere to put the Kosher for Pesach goods. This past year I was totally unprepared, and I ended up just leaving everything wrapped in a double layer of garbage bags until it was closer to Pesach and the shelves were ready. It was pretty inefficient. When you are making your purchases, don't forget to stock up on Windex and paper towels. This is my first point of discussion in Part I.

Order Necessary Kitchen Items

Did you have enough peelers last Pesach? Were your knives sharp enough? Did your matzah holder crack? Although the best time to order these items is right after the last Pesach, when it is fresh in your mind, it's not too late to order the necessary items now. Also, check your stock to confirm that you have enough two-gallon Ziplocs, disposable tins, and permanent markers on hand. You will need these items to make your cooking and storing most efficient.

Bonus—Clean Out Freezer Space and Buy Your Meat

If you want to be really prepared, you (or your cleaning person) can clean out space in your freezer, line it, and stock it with Kosher for Pesach meat. You can only do this once you've finished your menu (unless you just guess), but it will definitely make the 5 Days easier if all your frozen goods have been purchased.

Order Haggadahs

This is pretty self-explanatory. If you need new Haggadahs, order them now.

Order Afikoman Gifts

In our home, we got smart. We don't ask our kids what they want. We just order what we want them to have, in advance, and that's what they get. And this is the time that I order it.

New Toys for Pesach

If you are like me, you probably don't want to clean your kids' toys for Pesach. I find it's best not to own a lot of toys—this naturally eliminates the problem. Needless to say, you don't need very many toys for eight days of Yom Tov—some Magna-Tiles and Mega Bloks are really enough. I explained in Part I how to clean the toys you want to use, but now is a great time for buying one or two new Pesach toys if you wish.

ARRANGING FOR CLEANING HELP AND BABYSITTING

Ahh, remember the days pre-COVID when we had help cleaning for Pesach? Good. For the purpose of this section, let's assume those days have returned. Now, some of you might be thinking, "Really? I need to book my cleaners and sitters early?" And to you I respond, "Yes. Yes. Yes." The expression "You snooze, you lose" applies. Do not be part of the naive group who thinks that their hired help is loyal only to them. It is each woman for herself. Book them early and book them for every time you think you might need them. I cannot reiterate this strongly enough. This is not the time to think, "Maybe I can get away without the cleaning lady three days before Yom Tov." Wipe these foolish thoughts from your head. In the worst case, you can offer your friends extra help if you see you won't need your "extra" help. Listen to my wise advice…you have been warned.

Same with babysitters. Find the youngest girls of legal age who babysit (*read:* cheap) and book them now. Or, better yet, convince your own girls to run an Erev Pesach camp to make money, with the caveat that your younger children get to attend the camp for free. Don't worry that you won't have the help of your bigger girls at home. They can help you at night. Thank me later.

Now you are ready for the 5 Days. Remember, it *can* be done, and *you* can do it!

PART III

Basic Recipes and All-Important Lists

These recipes will simplify (and yummify) your Pesach. Special thanks to my incredible mother for so many of the recipes I make today! Friendly reminder: Double-check that all the ingredients you have purchased are Kosher for Pesach.

Main Dishes

Prize-Winning Potato Chip Schnitzel

(And you thought regular schnitzel was unhealthy!)

> 3 lbs. prepared chicken breast
> (sliced/cut/flattened—however you like it)
> 6 eggs
> 1 c. potato starch
> Large bag of regular or barbecue potato chips, crushed
> Oil for frying

Heat a large frying pan over high heat with oil about one-third of the way up the pan. Meanwhile, dip each piece of chicken breast in potato starch, then egg, and then crushed potato chips. Fry the chicken in oil, flipping after about 6 minutes. Drain onto a paper towel. This recipe can be made four days in advance, stored in the refrigerator, and reheated uncovered. In our home we serve this for lunch on Shabbos, and it is good, even heated on top of a *blech*.

London Broil

2.5 lbs. meat

5 garlic cloves, minced

¾ c. balsamic vinegar

¼ c. olive oil

Salt and pepper for searing

Make diagonal slits in the meat on both sides. Mix the garlic, vinegar, and olive oil together and pour over the meat. Marinate for three hours in the refrigerator. When the meat is ready, drain the excess liquid. Season it with salt and pepper and sear it in a frying pan until it is browned on both sides. Remove the meat from the pan, place it in a baking dish, and bake it at 450° for about 15 minutes, flipping halfway. If you like it more well done, keep it in for longer or switch the oven to a low broil for 4 minutes. Let cool before slicing.

Brisket #1

2.5–3 lbs. brisket

3 onions

6 garlic cloves, minced

¼ c. vinegar

½ c. water

¾ c. brown sugar

½ c. ketchup

Line a baking pan with onion and garlic gloves and place the meat on top. Mix together the vinegar, water, brown sugar, and ketchup and pour on top of the meat. Bake the brisket covered at 350° for about four hours or until the brisket is soft. Slice when cool.

Brisket #2

2.5–3 lbs. brisket

1 c. duck sauce

¼ c. brown sugar

⅓ c. sweet wine

1 squeeze ketchup

2 T. soy sauce

Mix together all the ingredients and pour them on top of the meat. Bake the brisket covered at 350° for about four hours or until the brisket is soft. Slice when cool.

Corned Beef

3 lbs. corned beef

2 T. oil

5 T. ketchup

2 T. vinegar

1 c. brown sugar

Boil the corned beef for three to four hours in a pot of boiling water until very soft. Remove the meat from the water and place in a baking pan. Mix the rest of the ingredients and pour them over the corned beef. Bake it in the oven for half an hour at 350°.

Chicken in Wine

2 onions, sliced into rings

Oil for sautéing

1 chicken, cut into eighths

1 c. potato starch

1 c. white wine

Salt

Pepper

Sauté the onions in a large pot until transparent. Meanwhile, mix the potato starch, salt, and pepper in a Ziploc and place each piece of chicken in the bag so that each piece is coated with starch. Add the chicken to the pot of onions and fry it until it is browned. Next, fill the pot with water till the chicken is generously covered and add one cup of wine. Cook it on the stovetop on a low flame for about two hours until the chicken is soft.

Soup Accompaniments

Matzah Balls

If you've ever tried making matzah balls from shemurah matzah meal, you might have had golf balls as your finished product. Well, not anymore. These matzah balls are perfect! The recipe was provided by Arthur Shattan of Portland with a slight addition by me (because you can't have matzah balls without cinnamon). They can be used with equal success with shemurah or non-shemurah matzah meal.

> 4 eggs
> ½ c. seltzer
> 6 T. oil
> 1 c. matzah meal
> Salt
> Pepper
> Garlic powder
> Cinnamon

Beat the eggs first! Then add the seltzer and oil, followed by the dry ingredients.

Refrigerate for an hour. When ready, form two-inch balls and drop into your soup, which should be simmering on a low to medium flame. Each batch makes fifteen matzah balls. This recipe can be multiplied and frozen in advance.

Side Dishes

Apple Kugel

10 apples, peeled and sliced

Cinnamon and sugar

5 eggs

1½ c. sugar

1½ t. baking powder

½ c. potato starch

¾ c. oil

¾ c. orange juice

1 t. vanilla

Place the apples in a baking pan and sprinkle them with cinnamon and sugar. Combine the rest of the ingredients and pour them over the apples. Bake at 350° for one hour covered and 15 minutes uncovered.

Onion Kugel

This is an amazing kugel—don't Pass It Over. Thank you to my sister-in-law Devorah for the recipe.

6 eggs, separated

6–8 onions

Oil to sauté

⅓ c. potato starch

⅓ c. oil

Salt

Pepper

Beat the egg whites until stiff. Sauté the onions in oil, let cool, and mix them with the yolks, potato starch, oil, salt, and pepper. Fold the egg whites into the mixture and pour it into a baking pan. Bake at 350° for about 45 minutes. Will look like a golden potato kugel when done.

Potato Kugel

5 lbs. potatoes

1 onion

6 eggs

1 c. oil

½ T. salt

Pepper

Peel the potatoes and the onion and cut them into a size that fits your food processor. Place them in a bowl of water. In another bowl mix the eggs, oil, salt, and pepper. Preheat the oven to 450°. Working quickly, grate the potatoes and the onion with the shredder blade of the food processor and drain any excess liquid. Empty the food processor bowl into the egg mixture and mix together well. Pour it all into a 9" x 13" baking pan and bake the kugel at 450° for 30 minutes and then at 350° for one hour. The kugel will look golden brown when ready.

Vegetable Kugel Gone Wrong

This recipe is supposed to serve as a kugel. Honestly, it is too liquidy, but I often make it because everyone (except my children) loves it. I serve it in a bowl and pretend it's a vegetable dish.

2 large onions, diced

1 package fresh mushrooms, sliced

6 zucchinis, peeled and sliced

Oil for sautéing

3 t. potato starch

3 t. margarine

1 c. mayonnaise

Salt and pepper to taste

Sauté the onions and mushrooms in oil until lightly browned and then add the zucchini. Add the remaining ingredients and stir until mixed. Pour the mixture into a 9" x 13" pan and bake at 350° for an hour.

Ratatouille

1 onion, diced

⅓ c. olive oil

4 cloves minced garlic

1½ eggplants, cubed

2 medium zucchinis, sliced

3 green peppers, sliced,

6 tomatoes, cubed

Salt, pepper, and basil to taste

In a large frying pan or wide pot, sauté the onion in olive oil and garlic. When translucent, add the eggplant, then sauté for 3 minutes. Add the zucchini and sauté for 3 minutes. Add the green peppers and sauté for 2 minutes. Mix well. Add the tomatoes and spices to taste, and enjoy!

Salads

I make all the dressings in advance for the entire Pesach, store them in the fridge, and use them as needed.

Coleslaw

2 bags coleslaw mix

½ c. lemon juice

1 t. salt

¾ c. sugar

7 T. mayonnaise

⅓ c. water

Marinate all the ingredients in a Ziploc bag. Add the coleslaw and mix three to four hours before the meal.

Chinese Cabbage Salad

During the year, I top this with sesame and sunflower seeds. On Pesach, you can top it with slivered almonds.

2 bags coleslaw mix

¾ c. sugar

½ c. vegetable oil

½ c. vinegar

¼ c. imitation soy sauce

Mix all the ingredients in a Ziploc bag. Add the coleslaw and mix three to four hours before the meal.

Salad Dressing

This is for any sweet spinach or lettuce salad (think mandarin oranges, mangos, pecans). Here are two options. Just mix the ingredients together.

Version #1

½ c. sugar

¾ c. oil

⅓ c. balsamic vinegar

1 t. salt

Version #2

1 c. oil

⅓ c. balsamic vinegar

¼ c. sugar

1 T. honey

½ t. salt

Cucumber Salad

6 cucumbers, peeled with alternate strokes and sliced thinly

Salt

1 onion, sliced

1 c. sugar

1 c. vinegar

½ c. water

Salt the sliced cucumbers for 10 minutes and then rinse off the salt. Add the remaining ingredients and marinate the salad. This will keep for a few days in the fridge.

Desserts

Classic Brownies

An oldie but a goodie.

½ c. cocoa

¾ c. oil

4 eggs

2 c. sugar

¾ c. potato starch

½ c. chocolate chips (add last after the rest is mixed)

Mix all the ingredients together in a bowl besides the chocolate chips. Add them in. Pour the batter into a 9" x 13" pan and bake for 30 minutes at 350°. Check for readiness with a toothpick.

Rocky Road Brownies

Warning—these are deadly! The recipe is in three parts.

A

1½ c. oil

3 c. sugar

4 t. vanilla

6 eggs

B

1½ c. potato starch

1 c. cocoa

¾ t. baking powder

¾ t. salt

C

1 bag chocolate chips

1 bag mini marshmallows

Mix the ingredients from group A, then add in the ingredients from group B and mix again. Last, fold in the ingredients from group C. Pour into a 9" x 13" pan and bake for 45 minutes at 350°.

Blondies

When you need something for Kiddush.

3 eggs

1 c. sugar

½ c. oil

3 T. water

2 c. matzah meal

1 c. chocolate chips (add last after the rest is mixed)

Mix all the ingredients together in a bowl besides the chocolate chips. Add them in. Pour the batter into a 9" x 13" pan and bake for 30 minutes at 350°. Check for readiness with a toothpick.

Chocolate Chip Biscotti

These are a real family favorite. They are even better when served frozen. This recipe is reprinted from Passover by Design by Susie Fishbein, with permission of the author.

2 c. sugar

1 c. (2 sticks) margarine

6 large eggs

2¾ cups matzah cake meal

¾ c. potato starch

½ t. fine sea salt

1 c. walnuts, finely chopped

2 c. semi-sweet chocolate chips

2 t. sugar

1 t. cinnamon

Cover two cookie sheets with parchment paper or spray with nonstick cooking spray and set aside.

In the bowl of a mixer, cream the two cups of sugar and margarine. Beat until light and fluffy. Add the eggs one at a time and continue beating.

In a medium bowl, whisk together the matzah cake meal, potato starch, salt, and walnuts. Add to the egg mixture in three additions, stirring between additions. Stir in the chocolate chips by hand.

Divide the dough in half and place on the prepared cookie sheets. Shape each half into a large rectangle, approximately 7" x 11". You may need to lightly wet your hands to prevent them from sticking to the dough.

In a small bowl, combine the two teaspoons of sugar with the cinnamon. Sprinkle on top of each loaf. Bake at 350° for 50 minutes. Remove from the oven and let stand for 5 minutes. Cut into individual biscotti while warm. Cool completely.

Lemon Freeze

The dessert for when you want to pretend you're eating healthy.

4 eggs, separated

1 8-oz. container frozen whipped topping

1 c. sugar

⅓ c. lemon juice

Separate the eggs and beat the egg whites until they are stiff. In a separate bowl, mix the rest of the ingredients. Fold the egg whites into the second bowl. Freeze.

Option: You can freeze these in muffin papers in muffin tins. When you are ready to serve, pop them out of the paper and serve them upside down.

Chocolate Mousse Pie

7 oz. chocolate chips

½ c. or 1 stick (unsalted) margarine

7 eggs

1 c. sugar

1 t. vanilla

1 8 oz. whipped topping

Melt the chocolate and the margarine in a pot over a low flame and then remove from fire.

At the same time, separate the eggs. Beat the egg whites until they are stiff and then add the sugar and vanilla. Add the egg yolks to the cooled chocolate. Fold the chocolate into the egg white mixture. Pour two-thirds of the mousse batter into a 9" x 13" pan and bake it in the oven at 325° for 30 minutes. Refrigerate the rest. When the cake is cooled, pour the cooled mousse on top. Freeze. At a later time, layer the dessert with beaten whipped topping.

Classic Chocolate Mousse

¾ bag chocolate chips (9 oz.)

2 sticks (1 c.) unsalted margarine

6 eggs

¾ c. sugar

Melt the margarine and chocolate in a pot over a low flame and then remove from fire. At the same time, separate the eggs. Beat the egg whites until they are stiff and then add the sugar. Add the egg yolks to the cooled chocolate. Fold the chocolate into the egg white mixture. Refrigerate for 30 minutes. Pour into pans and freeze until ready to serve.

Ice Cream

6 eggs, separated

1 c. sugar

1 16-oz. container frozen whipped topping

1 t. vanilla

Separate the eggs. In a large bowl, beat the egg whites until stiff and then add the sugar. In a second bowl, beat the whipped topping until it peaks and then add vanilla. Combine the mixtures in both bowls. Discard the yolks. Freeze.

Variations of Ice Cream

Vanilla Ice Cream:
Don't do anything else, but if you like, you can add chocolate syrup or chocolate chips. (Chocolate chips should be added to everything!)

Chocolate Ice Cream:
Add cocoa as desired.

Rainbow Ice Cream:

Add in a container of sprinkles. (In my humble opinion, this is gross, but my kids love it, so I make it once a year.)

Coffee Ice Cream:

Dilute 2 tablespoons of coffee granules in hot water and pour into the mixture. Add more as desired.

Chocolate Chip Cookies

>2 c. matzah farfel
>
>1 c. ground nuts
>
>2 c. matzah meal
>
>1½ c. sugar
>
>4 eggs
>
>⅔ c. oil
>
>Pinch salt
>
>1 c. chocolate chips

Mix together all the ingredients in a bowl and then fold in the chocolate chips. Drop spoonfuls of "dough" on a cookie sheet and bake at 350° for approximately 20 minutes.

Crunchy Cookies

These are amazing and "healthy" with all the nuts. Beware—they get eaten quickly!

>6 oz. ground almonds
>
>6 oz. ground walnuts
>
>2 eggs
>
>1½ c. sugar
>
>2 c. potato starch
>
>¾ c. oil
>
>¼ c. orange juice
>
>3 T. vanilla sugar
>
>10 oz. chocolate chips

Mix together all the ingredients in a bowl and then fold in the chocolate chips. Refrigerate the dough for a few hours. Preheat the oven to 350°. Roll the dough into one-inch round balls and place them two inches apart on a cookie sheet. Bake for 20–25 minutes until lightly golden brown. Makes approximately forty-eight cookies.

ALL-IMPORTANT LISTS

Sample Shopping List

(Courtesy of Jamie Geller)

A note from Meira: Please remember to check your products for a reliable Kosher for Passover symbol! Or check oukosher.org for items that don't need a special Kosher for Passover symbol. Before you head out to shop, check your menu and note all the ingredients that you will need. (I personally recommend freezing your extra spices from year to year so you don't have to keep buying them again.)

Matzah Products

- Matzah
- Matzah meal
- Cake meal

Spices

- Salt
- Pepper
- Paprika
- Cinnamon
- Oregano
- Basil
- Garlic powder
- Parsley flakes/frozen cubes
- Dill
- Soup powder

Baking

- Baking powder
- Baking soda
- Cacao/cocoa powder
- Sugar
- Potato starch
- Vanilla extract

Oil/Vinegar

- Extra virgin olive oil
- Walnut oil
- Canola oil (Sephardim only)
- Coconut oil
- Balsamic vinegar
- Red/white wine vinegar
- Apple cider vinegar
- Bottled salad dressing

Dry/Canned Ingredients

- Quinoa (those that use it on Pesach)
- Rice (Sephardim only)
- Canned tuna
- Marinara sauce
- Tomato paste
- Jelly
- Canned fruits or veggies
- Kosher for Passover cereal
- Chips
- Coffee
- Tea
- Nuts
- Chocolate chips
- Honey
- Pickles
- Olives

Beverages

- Wine
- Grape juice
- Juice
- Bottled water (for outings)

For the Fridge

- Cheese
- Butter/margarine
- Milk
- Sour cream
- Eggs
- Frozen whip
- Fresh/frozen meat and chicken
- Fresh/frozen fish (gefilte fish is a favorite!)
- And, of course, don't forget the fresh fruits and veggies!

LIST OF IMPORTANT KITCHEN ITEMS

- Sharp knives
- Chicken shears
- Multiple peelers (so your kids can help)
- Crock-pot (and liners)
- Hand or stand electric mixer
- Food processor
- Good electric carving knife
- Very large frying pan for both meat (to fry schnitzel) and dairy (to make *matzah brei*)
- Shabbos *blech*
- Immersion blender (if you purée a lot of soups)
- Hot water urn
- Miscellaneous kitchen items (spatula, corkscrew, can opener)
- Mixing bowls (these can double as fruit bowls and salad bowls)
- Supplies for lining shelves
- Disposables for baking, serving, and storing
- Baby bottle (if relevant)

Rabbi Scheinberg's Pesach Cleaning List

Edited by Rabbi Moshe Finkelstein, Kiryat Mattersdorf, Jerusalem
Pesach 5765, Print Version
Reprinted with permission from www.orchos.org

These notes are based on the responsa of Moreinu v'Rabbeinu HaGaon Harav Chaim Pinchas Scheinberg, zt"l, Rosh Yeshivas Torah Ore, to questions posed by women who attended his regular talks. They have been compiled by a group of his students. The notes also include Hebrew sources and footnotes, which are not reproduced here.

CLEAN FOR PESACH AND ENJOY THE SEDER!

Preface

In former times, wealthy people who had large houses also had many servants who did their bidding, while poor people, who could not afford servants, lived in small homes with one or two rooms. Understandably, the pre-Passover chores of the rich were performed by the servants, while the poor, who had only their one or two rooms to clean, a few pieces of furniture, a minimum of utensils, and some clothing, took care of their needs themselves.

In those days, cleaning was hard. Tables were made of raw wood, requiring them to be scrubbed or even to be shaven to ensure that no pieces of food were hidden in the cracks. Earthen or wooden floors also needed to be thoroughly cleaned and scrubbed.

Today, we seem to be caught in a trap. The average modern home is larger than formerly. Furniture, utensils, and clothing are much more plentiful. The average home today can compare with the more affluent homes of previous generations. However, we do not have the servants that they had, so today, all the chores fall on the woman of the home. At the same time, she still feels obligated to clean and scrub as they did formerly, even though she has laminated furniture and tiled floors, making this type of cleaning unnecessary.

As a result of this, the pressure of pre-Pesach cleaning has reached unnecessary and overwhelming levels. The housewife often becomes overly nervous, unable to enjoy the holiday joy of Passover and unable to perform the mitzvos and obligations of the Seder night.

Introduction

Passover, like every other Yom Tov, must be enjoyed by every member of the family, including women. This is an obligation clearly defined in the Torah, as explained by our Sages. We can understand a person dreading Tishah B'Av, but Pesach is to be looked forward to and anticipated with joy. Every woman should be well-rested, relaxed, and alert at the Seder table so that she can fulfill all the Torah and Rabbinic obligations and follow the Haggadah with the rest of the family. Clearly, the performance of her pre-Passover duties must be balanced against her Passover obligations. Pre-Passover cleaning is required to avoid the danger of transgressing any Torah or Rabbinic prohibition of having chometz in the house on Pesach. It is evident from the responsa of the Rosh Hayeshiva, zt"l, that this need not be excessive.

It is not the intention here to abolish traditions that have been passed down by Klal Yisroel from generation to generation. Nevertheless, some practices adopted by women in the Passover cleaning today are not an actual continuation of the old traditions. For example, if a person does not sell his chometz, of course it is necessary to check his utensils and to wash off any chometz left on them, or to render the chometz inedible. But if the chometz is sold, then washing the pots, pans, and dishes that are going to be locked away is not necessary. One might be tempted to insist on doing the extra work any-way—to be *machmir*. However, in these stringencies lies the grave danger of causing many laxities and brushing aside many mitzvos completely, including Torah and Rabbinic obligations that women are required to do on Passover and particularly during the Seder. Many women like to do more "cleaning" than the bare minimum, to such an extent that some even incorporate their general "spring clean-ing" into their required pre-Passover chores. These extra exertions should not prevent them from fulfilling their obligations on Passover, and particularly on the Seder night.

General Notes

A. All property and possessions must be cleaned and checked to make sure that they are free of all chometz (except in the fol-lowing cases).

B. If, during the year, chometz is not brought into a place, that place does not have to be cleaned out or checked for chometz.

C. Any article which is not used on Pesach does not need to be checked for chometz, provided it is put away properly and the chometz in it is sold.

D. Crumbs that have been rendered completely inedible [*C. J. Weisberg explains:* by coating with small amount of household cleaner] to the extent that they are not fit to be eaten by a dog are not considered chometz.

E. The general obligation to check for and destroy crumbs does not apply if the crumbs are less than a *k'zayis* and are dirty or spoiled enough to prevent a person from eating them.

F. The household cleaner used (mentioned above and below) must spoil the crumbs slightly to the extent that people would refrain from eating them.

G. It is customary that any item to be kashered should not be used for 24 hours prior to *kashering*, in order that it should not be a *ben-yomo*.

Practical Applications

1. **Clothing closets:** If there is some significant possibility that chometz went into them, they should be checked for fully edible crumbs of chometz, besides large pieces of chometz. If the probability that chometz entered these places is remote, a *rav* can be consulted to clarify the conditions under which they do not have to be checked. This includes chests, dressers, basements, and all other similar places (see General Note E above).

2. **Floors:** We don't have earthen floors with deep cracks in them. It is sufficient for tiled or covered floors to be swept and washed with a household floor cleaner. Cracks and spaces between tiles do not have to be checked if the cleaning solution reaches into them.

3. **Food Cabinets:** If the cabinet is not going to be used on Passover, then you just have to lock it or seal it in a manner that will remind you not to use it on Passover, and sell it with the chometz (see General Notes C and E above). If the cabinet is going to be used on Pesach, take out all the food and wash it with a rag soaked in a household cleaner. Be sure the cleansing agent reaches into all the cracks and soaks into any crumbs that might be left there. The usual practice is to line the cabinets.

4. **Refrigerator:** Take the food out and wash the fridge with a rag soaked in a household cleaner. The racks are usually covered. (It is advisable to leave holes for air circulation.)

5. *Kashering* **sinks:** Clean the sinks (see General Note G), and pour a kettle of boiling water into them and on their sides. Some people pour hot water mixed with bleach down the drain. The usual practice today is to use an insert or line the sinks (e.g., aluminum foil, contact paper). If not difficult, this practice should be followed. **Faucets (Taps):** Cleaning, without any other *kashering* procedure, is sufficient.

6. **Marble and stainless-steel counters:** If they were used for hot chometz, they should first be cleaned well. They should either be completely covered so that nothing Pesach'dik touches them,

or (if it will not ruin the countertop) pour boiling hot water on them (see General Note G). Many people do both.

7. **Tabletops:** Wash them with a household cleaner. The usual practice is to cover the tables.

8. *Kashering* **Range/Oven/Stovetop:** Wash the top and side surface areas with a rag soaked in a strong household cleaner. Clean the knobs well. Grates can be kashered by first cleaning them well (see General Note G). Put them back on the stove, and then light all the burners, raising them to their maximum heat, and put a blech on top while the burners are on. This spreads the heat over the whole top and intensifies the heat on the grates. Let it burn for 5–10 minutes. [Be careful that the knobs don't melt.] After *kashering*, the usual practice today is to cover the stove-top with aluminum foil (being extremely careful not to block the air inlets around the burners and on the back of the stove, as this could create poisonous fumes in the room).

   Oven: If you want to use the oven: (a) First clean the oven well with an oven cleaner (e.g., Easy-Off). Make sure that it reaches into all the cracks and around the screws. (After using the oven cleaner, there is no need for further cleaning; see General Note G.) Then heat the inside of the oven by turning the oven on to its highest temperature for about one hour. (b) If your oven has a turbo option (a fan which circulates the heat), consult a *rav* about the particular type. (c) After *kashering*, if the oven door has a glass window, preferably cover the entire inside of the door with aluminum foil. (d) If a closed oven insert is available, this would be preferable. In this case, only washing and cleaning are necessary. (e) Do not use the chometz'dik oven racks for Pesach. If this is difficult, then one can *kasher* the racks with the same procedure as for the oven, placing them as close as possible to the heating element.

   If the oven is not going to be used: None of the above is necessary. Just make certain that there is no edible chometz inside, tape it closed well, and see #10 below.

9. **Pots, Pans, Dishes, and Silverware (Cutlery):** Whatever is not going to be used for Pesach should either be locked up or put away and sealed in a manner that will remind you not to use them on Pesach. If there is a possibility of actual chometz in them, the chometz should be sold (see General Note C). If you do not sell chometz, then they should be either washed or soaked in a household cleaner; it is not necessary to scrub them. (Concerning *kashering* utensils for Pesach, consult a *rav*.)

10. **Food Processor/Mixer:** A *rav* should be consulted.

11. **Dish Towels:** If one does not have a Pesach'dik set of dish towels, then one's regular dish towels may be used if they are washed with a detergent and no food remains attached to them. (It is customary to have a set of Pesach'dik dish towels.)

12. **Pesach Tablecloths:** These can be ironed with the same iron as is used during the rest of the year.

13. **Clothes, Blankets, Pockets, Etc.:** If they have been washed in detergent or dry cleaned, then there is no need for them to be checked (see General Note E). Otherwise, they need to be cleaned and checked thoroughly by brushing or shaking them out well. However, if there is a possibility of crumbs between the stitches or in a hidden crevice, which cannot be shaken out, then they must be wiped with a rag that has been soaked in a detergent. Clothes that will not be worn on Pesach do not have to be checked, but they should be put away and the chometz in them sold (see General Notes C and # 10 on Pots and Pans).

14. **Siddurim, Benchers, Seforim, Books:** If there is a chance that they contain chometz, then they should either be put away and sold with other chometz utensils (see General Notes C) or cleaned and checked well.

15. **Toys:** If there is edible chometz, then it should be either removed or rendered inedible (see General Notes E). There is no need to scrub them.

16. **Techina and Other Kitniyos (Legumes):** May be used after the house has been cleaned for Pesach. They should not be cooked

in utensils that will be used on Pesach, and certainly not on Pesach itself (according to the Ashkenazic minhag).

17. **Last-Minute Preparations:** For example, setting the table, etc., should be completed early enough in the day so that you will be able to rest a little bit. Be ready to start the Seder immediately after *Maariv*, to ensure that the children won't fall asleep at the Seder.

ENJOY PESACH! Try to make the Pesach chores easy for yourself. Don't do unnecessary hard work. Don't do unnecessary cleaning. You can be like a Queen, and you must enjoy your Pesach!

How to Make the Seder Enjoyable for Your Kids

THERE IS SO MUCH work that goes into making the Seder that we often miss the point.

The Seder is an incredible opportunity, and it comes only once a year. Even though, as Jews, we constantly try to strengthen our faith, the Seder night affords us the opportunity to do so with complete focus. We recount the miracles Hashem did for us and affirm that He has never forsaken us and never will forsake us.

There is an additional dimension that makes the Seder unique from other mitzvos. "And you shall tell your child on that day as follows: 'Because of this, Hashem did for me, when he took me out of Egypt'" (*Shemos* 13:8). As we solidify our faith on the Seder night, we give that faith over to our children. We ignore the grape juice spills and the afikomen bidding wars. We praise great questions, even if they are simple, and reward participation, if only for a short span. We never raise our voice and we ignore snide remarks. The Seder night is not about the food or the company; it is about our faith and the faith of our children. And we do our best to remain focused on the task at hand.

We try to keep the kids engaged throughout, using props and decoration to liven up the experience. We purchase Haggadahs with larger-than-life illustrations to keep the children interested. We look into the past and future simultaneously and tell a story that interweaves the generations. We shine a light in the darkness and pave a way for our future.

L'shanah haba'ah b'Yerushalayim!

Glossary

batel: nullified.

blech: warming plate.

kasher: clean and cover, in order to make usable for Passover.

k'zayis: size of an olive.

l'kavod Yom Tov: in honor of the holiday.

machmir: stringent.

mechiras chametz: halachic sale of chametz.

Notes

Notes

Notes

Notes

Notes

About the Author

MEIRA SPIVAK is the director of Oregon NCSY, where she has developed Jewish educational programming for teens and parents for fourteen years. She also serves as the director of Camp Kesher, a growing summer camp in the Pacific Northwest. She has a master's degree in Jewish Education from Touro College and is an emerging leader in the application of the Systematic Inventive Thinking (SIT) method of creativity, cofounded by Jacob Goldenberg. Based upon SIT leadership practice, Meira facilitates workshops and training to help businesses achieve desired results. In the past, Meira was a caterer, owned a gift basket business, and was an aerobics instructor. As the mother of a large family, Meira understands the stresses of everyday life—and sees the humor in them.